A Note to Parents and Teachers

DK READERS is a compelling reading programme for children, designed in conjunction with leading literacy experts, including Cliff Moon M.Ed., Honorary Fellow of the University of Reading. Cliff Moon has spent many years as a teacher and teacher educator specializing in reading and has written more than 140 books for children and teachers. He reviews regularly for teachers' journals.

Beautiful illustrations and superb full-colour photographs combine with engaging, easy-to-read stories to offer a fresh approach to each subject in the series. Each DK READER is guaranteed to capture a child's interest while developing his or her reading skills, general knowledge, and love of reading.

The four levels of DK READERS are aimed at different reading abilities, enabling you to choose the books that are exactly right for your child:

Level 1 – Beginning to read
Level 2 – Beginning to read alone
Level 3 – Reading alone
Level 4 – Proficient readers

The "normal" age at which a child begins to read can be anywhere from three to eight years old, so these levels are only a general guideline.

No matter which level you select, you can be sure th
child lear

LONDON, NEW YORK, MUNICH, PARIS,
MELBOURNE and DELHI

Project Editors Anna Lofthouse
Naia Bray Moffatt
Series Editor Deborah Lock
Senior Art Editor Cheryl Telfer
Art Editor Catherine Goldsmith
Production Shivani Pandey
DTP Designer Almudena Diaz
Jacket Designer Dean Price
Picture Researcher Angela Anderson
Photographer Bill Ling

Reading Consultant
Cliff Moon M.Ed.

Published in Great Britain by
Dorling Kindersley Limited,
80, The Strand, London WC2R 0RL

10 9

A CIP catalogue record for this book is
available from the British Library.

ISBN-13: 978-0-7513-4620-6

Colour reproduction by Colourscan, Singapore
Printed and bound in China by L Rex Printing Co., Ltd.

The publisher would like to thank the following for
their kind permission to reproduce their images:
Position key: c=centre; b=bottom; l=left; r=right; t=top
Getty Images: Vince Streano 8-9. **Masterfile UK**: Daryl Benson 25;
Greg Stott 24. **Zefa Picture Library**: 11; 16-17.
Jarrold Publishing at Woburn Safari, courtesy of the Marquess of
Tavistock and the Trustees of the Bedford Estates Park: 12-13c;/
All other photographs taken at Woburn Safari Park, courtesy of the
Marquess of Tavistock and the Trustees of the Bedford Estates
Models: Billy Ling, Matt Ling, Terrie Ling
Illustrations: Venice Shone

All other images © Dorling Kindersley.
For further information see: www.dkimages.com

see our complete
catalogue at

www.dk.com

 **READERS**

 BEGINNING 1 TO READ

A Trip to the Zoo

Written by Karen Wallace

A Dorling Kindersley Book

Billy was a boy
who loved animals.
He read books about them and
he watched films about them.

In the holidays, Billy's mum
had a surprise for him and
his little brother, Matt.
It was a trip to the zoo.

Billy and Matt were very excited.
First, they saw a huge elephant
who was having her
teeth checked.

Then the elephant
walked around slowly
to let the children stroke her.
"Her skin feels so hairy,"
said Matt.

"Look at the rhinos," Billy said.
"Their horns look very sharp,"
Matt replied.

horn

Billy told Matt that rhinos
may seem clumsy, but
they can run very fast.

"Look! Those horses have stripes,"
said Matt.
"Those are not horses,"
said Billy.
"They're zebras."

"Can you ride a zebra?"
asked Matt.
"No, zebras are wild animals."

stripes

"Here are some more
striped animals," called Matt.
Billy looked at the tigers
lying under the tree.

They looked so peaceful.
It was hard for him to believe
that tigers are fierce hunters
in the wild.

Chomp!

Chomp!

"No stripes this time, Matt,"
Billy said.
"Giraffes have
big and small patches."

Matt was feeling hungry.
"I think the giraffes
are hungry too!" said Billy.

patches

Next, they went to the ape house.
"Look – that gorilla is
taking care of her baby,"
said Matt.

It was time to go
to the sea lion show.
But Billy did not want to.
He was staring at the
gorilla's big nostrils!

nostril

The sea lion show began.
The sea lion came up and
touched a fish with its nose.

nose

Plop! Plop!

The sea lion gobbled the fish
and dived back into the water.

Billy and Matt looked through the underground window at the pool.

They watched a sea lion use
its flippers to swim underwater.

flipper

After lunch, they went to see
the squirrel monkeys.
"Where are they?" asked Matt.
"Look up in the trees," said Mum.

They were running through the
branches and one was hanging
upside down by its tail!

tail

"Look, those koalas are climbing trees, too," said Matt. "Their sharp claws help them to grip," Billy explained. "Hold on tight, baby koala!" called Matt.

claws

Some furry wallabies
hopped by.
"They are like kangaroos
but smaller," said Billy.
"Watch me jump
like a wallaby,"
said Matt.

Boing!
Boing!
Boing!

"I wish we could take
some animals home," said Billy.
"I'm afraid we can't do that,"
said Mum.

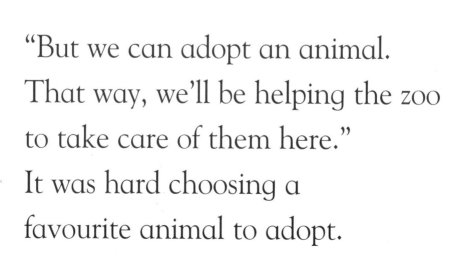

"But we can adopt an animal.
That way, we'll be helping the zoo
to take care of them here."
It was hard choosing a
favourite animal to adopt.

When they got home,
Billy and Matt
started making
a thank-you surprise
for Mum...

They painted pictures
of all the animals
they had seen.
"Now we have
a zoo at home!"
said Billy.

Picture word list

 horn
page 8

 nose
page 18

stripes
page 10

flipper
page 21

 patches
page 15

tail
page 23

 nostril
page 16

claws
page 25